ILLUSTRATED CLASSIC
Christmas Carols

Compiled by Katie Warner
Illustrated by Adalee Hude

TAN Books
Gastonia, North Carolina

Illustrated Classic Christmas Carols © 2025 Katie Warner

All rights reserved. With the exception of short excerpts used in critical review, no part of this work may be reproduced, transmitted, or stored in any form whatsoever, without the prior written permission of the publisher. Creation, exploitation, and distribution of any unauthorized editions of this work, in any format in existence now or in the future—including but not limited to text, audio, and video—is prohibited without the prior written permission of the publisher.

All sheet music in this edition is in the Public Domain via sources such as hymnary.org and openhymnal.org.

Unless otherwise noted, The Revised Standard Version of the Bible: Catholic Edition, copyright © 1965, 1966 the Division of Christian Education of the National Council of the Churches of Christ in the United States of America. Used by permission. All rights reserved.

Front cover, interior design, and illustrations by Adalee Hude

Typesetting by Jordan Avery

ISBN: 978-1-5051-3486-5
Kindle ISBN: 978-1-5051-3721-7
ePUB ISBN: 978-15051-3720-0

Published in the United States by
TAN Books
PO Box 269
Gastonia, NC 28053

www.TANBooks.com

Printed in India

Contents

Introduction 1

Angels We Have Heard on High 2

Away in a Manger 4

God Rest Ye Merry, Gentlemen 6

Hark! The Herald Angels Sing 8

In the Bleak Midwinter 10

It Came upon the Midnight Clear 12

Joy to the World 14

O Come, All Ye Faithful (*Adeste Fideles*) 16

O Come, O Come, Emmanuel (*Veni, Veni Emmanuel*) 18

O Holy Night 20

O Little Town of Bethlehem 22

Once in Royal David's City 24

Silent Night 26

The First Noel 28

What Child Is This? 30

We Three Kings of Orient Are 32

Arise, all ye nobles and peasants; Mary invites all, rich and poor, just and sinners, to enter the cave of Bethlehem, to adore and to kiss the feet of her new-born Son.... Let us enter; let us not be afraid.

—St. Alphonsus Liguori

Introduction

It's that wonderful time in the liturgical year again: the hopeful anticipation of Advent, followed by the mystical joy of the Christ Child's coming at Christmas.

May this collection of artwork, reflections, and hymns help prepare a place in your heart for Our Lord to dwell this holy season. Whether you sing these hymns as a family by your table or tree, with a group of carolers in neighborhoods or nursing homes, or with your parish as you prepare for and ponder the Incarnation together, let the words sink deep and your voice raise high as we share with our dark world the good news that Christ has come to save us.

I truly hope this book becomes a treasured resource for you! Know that you are in my prayers, this holy season and always.

Katie Warner

Angels We Have Heard on High

Traditional French carol
English translation by
Bishop James Chadwick, 1862

Can you imagine the scene? Angels blanketing the sky, their voices filling the air with praise and song. Creation itself—even the mountains—seems to burst with joy over the Savior's birth. Will you answer the invitation to "Come to Bethlehem, and see"? Join the shepherds in adoring the newborn Christ, here lying in a manger, and raise your voice with joy over the Incarnation: God has become man, and nothing will ever be the same.

1. An - gels we have heard on high, Sweet - ly sing - ing o'er the plains,
2. Shep - herds, why this ju - bi - lee? Why your joy - ous strains pro - long?
3. Come to Beth - le - hem and see Christ Whose birth the an - gels sing;
4. See Him in a man - ger laid, Whom the choirs of an - gels praise;

And the moun - tains in re - ply E - cho - ing their joy - ous strains.
What the glad - some ti - dings be Which in - spire your heav'n - ly song?
Come, a - dore on bend - ed knee, Christ the Lord, the new - born King.
Ma - ry, Jo - seph, lend your aid, While our hearts in love we raise.

Glo - - - - - - - - ri - a, in ex - cel - sis De - o!

Glo - - - - - - - - ri - a, in ex - cel - sis De - o!

Away in a Manger

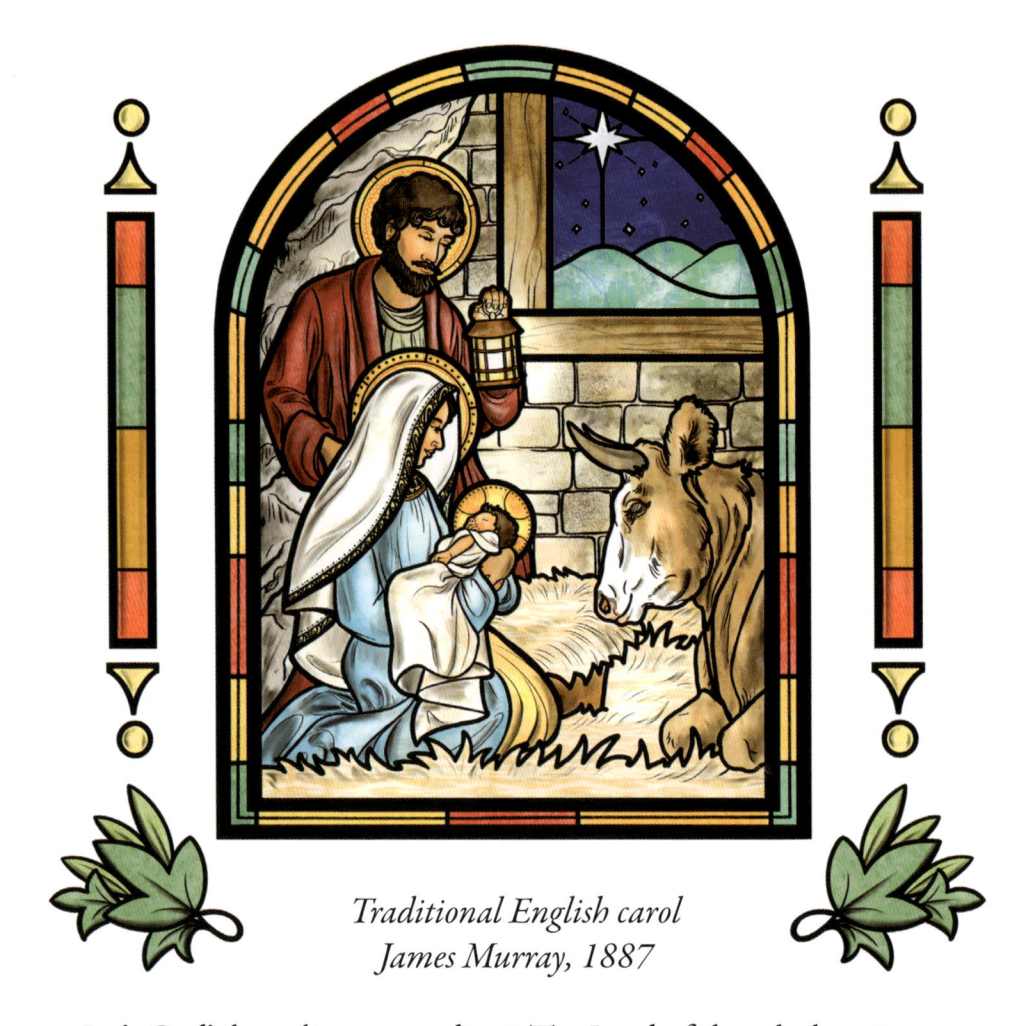

Traditional English carol
James Murray, 1887

Isn't God's humility astounding? The Lord of the whole universe lowered Himself, becoming a *baby*, born in meager conditions, and like us in all things except sin (see Heb 4:15). Don't just sing, but sincerely pray the words of the last stanza, asking for the Child Jesus to bless you this Christmas and to make your heart humble like His, fit for heaven.

1. A-way in a man-ger, no crib for a bed, The lit-tle Lord
2. The cat-tle are low-ing, the Ba-by a-wakes, But lit-tle Lord
3. Be near me, Lord Je-sus, I ask Thee to stay Close by me for-

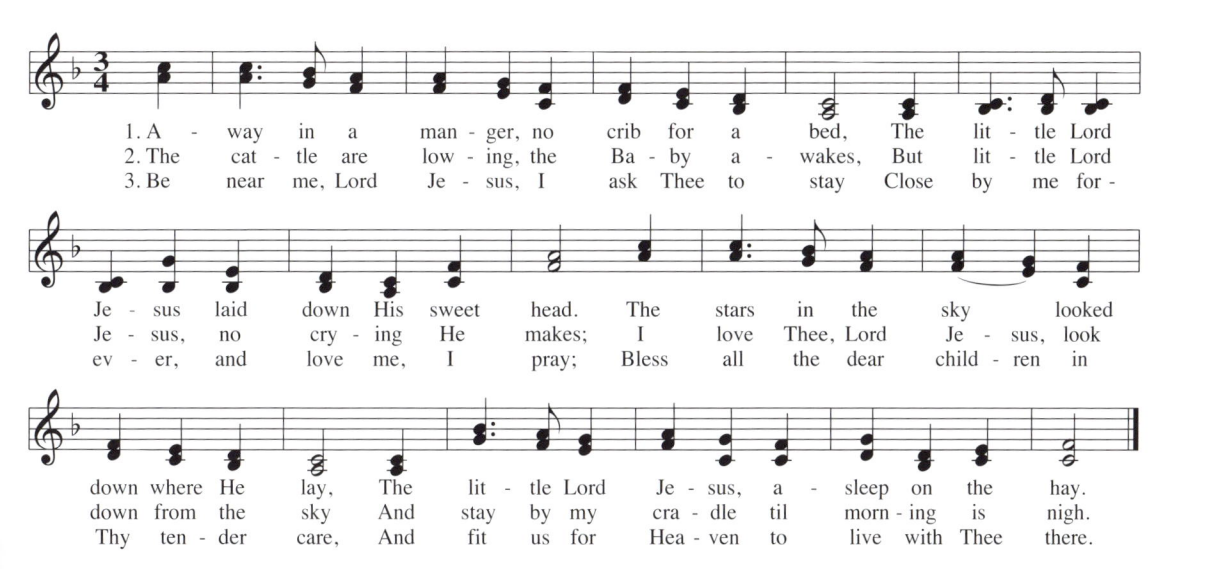

Je-sus laid down His sweet head. The stars in the sky looked
Je-sus, no cry-ing He makes; I love Thee, Lord Je-sus, look
ev-er, and love me, I pray; Bless all the dear child-ren in

down where He lay, The lit-tle Lord Je-sus, a-sleep on the hay.
down from the sky And stay by my cra-dle til morn-ing is nigh.
Thy ten-der care, And fit us for Hea-ven to live with Thee there.

God Rest Ye Merry, Gentlemen

English carol, 18th Century

Isaiah chapter 40 begins: "Comfort, comfort my people . . ." And what long-awaited comfort and joy has now entered the world in Christ Jesus, Our Savior. The second part of the book of Isaiah is often referred to as the "Book of Consolation," because it describes Yahweh's saving action. This hymn, likewise, reminds us that Christ has come to free us from Satan's power. May we rest in that comfort and *good news*, and may we continue to find and rejoice in the freedom of Christ's victory over sin.

1. God rest ye merry, gentlemen, let nothing you dismay,
   Remember Christ our Savior was born on Christmas Day;
   To save us all from Satan's pow'r when we were gone astray.
   O tidings of comfort and joy, comfort and joy; O tidings of comfort and joy.

2. From God our heav'nly Father a blessed angel came;
   And unto certain shepherds brought tidings of the same;
   How that in Bethlehem was born the Son of God by name.
   O tidings of comfort and joy, comfort and joy; O tidings of comfort and joy.

3. "Fear not, then," said the angel, "Let nothing you afright
   This day is born a Savior of a pure Virgin bright,
   To free all those who trust in Him from Satan's pow'r and might."
   O tidings of comfort and joy, comfort and joy; O tidings of comfort and joy.

4. The shepherds at those tidings rejoiced much in mind,
   And left their flocks a-feeding in tempest, storm and wind,
   And went to Beth'lem straightaway this blessed Babe to find.
   O tidings of comfort and joy, comfort and joy; O tidings of comfort and joy.

5. Now to the Lord sing praises all you within this place,
   And with true love and brotherhood each other now embrace;
   This holy tide of Christmas all others doth deface.

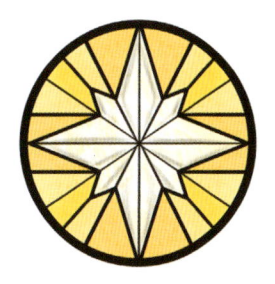

Hark! The Herald Angels Sing

Charles Wesley, 1739

Notice the all-encompassing focus of Christ's coming and mission in the verses of this hymn: angels . . . us . . . *everyone* (light and life to *all* He brings). Jesus tells us in the Gospel that He came to draw all to Himself (see Jn 12:32). As you sing here of Christ's Incarnation, birth, ministry, and salvific purpose, pray that all will truly come to know and love Christ, who came to be with us on earth, so that we may someday be with Him forever in heaven.

1. Hark! The her - ald an - gels sing, "Glo - ry to the new - born King;
2. Christ, by high - est Heav'n a - dored; Christ the ev - er - last - ing Lord;
3. Hail the heav'n - ly Prince of Peace! Hail the Sun of Right - eous - ness!

Peace on earth, and mer - cy mild, God and sin - ners re - con - ciled!"
Late in time, be - hold Him come, Off - spring of a vir - gin's womb.
Light and life to all He brings, Ris'n with heal - ing in His wings.

Joy - ful, all ye na - tions rise, Join the tri - umph of the skies;
Veiled in flesh the God - head see; Hail th'in - car - nate De - i - ty,
Mild He lays His glo - ry by, Born that man no more may die.

With th'an - gel - ic host pro - claim, "Christ is born in Beth - le - hem!"
Pleased with us in flesh to dwell, Je - sus our Em - man - u - el.
Born to raise the sons of earth, Born to give them se - cond birth.

Hark! the her - ald an - gels sing, "Glo - ry to the new - born King!"

9

In the Bleak Midwinter

Christina Rosetti, 1872

Notice the contrasts in this beautiful song: the cold, bleakness of winter meets the warmth and light of Christ; the glory of heaven descends to the poverty of earth. God has lavished us with more than we could ever repay. But He longs for one thing from us: our love.

1. In the bleak mid-winter, frost-y wind made moan,
2. Our God, Heav'n can-not hold Him, nor earth sus-tain;
3. E-nough for Him, whom cher-u-bim, wor-ship night and day,
4. An-gels and arch-an-gels may have ga-thered there,
5. What can I give Him, poor as I am?

Earth stood hard as i - ron, wa-ter like a stone;
Heav'n and earth shall flee a - way when He comes to reign.
Breast-ful of milk, and a man-ger-ful of hay; En-
Cher-u-bim and ser-a-phim thronged the air;
If I were a shep-herd, I would bring a lamb;

Snow had fall-en, snow on snow, snow on snow on snow,
In the bleak mid-win-ter a sta-ble place suf-ficed
ough for Him, whom an-gels fall down be-fore,
But His mo-ther on - ly, in her mai-den bliss,
If I were a Wise Man, I would do my part;

In the bleak mid-win-ter, long a - go.
The Lord God Al-migh-ty, Je - sus Christ.
Ox and ass and ca-mel which a - dore.
Wor-shiped the be-lov - ed with a kiss.
Yet what can I give Him: give my heart.

11

It Came upon the Midnight Clear

Edmund Sears, 1849

The adjectives this carol uses to describe the world are stark: solemn, weary, sad, lowly, Babel, crushing, toil, painful, ever-circling. But notice the angels above, singing into this place of heaviness, reminding us that our God has come to bring peace, and He will make all things new (see Rv 21:5).

1. It came upon the midnight clear, That glorious song of old, From
2. Still through the cloven skies they come With peaceful wings unfurled, And
3. Yet with the woes of sin and strife The world has suffered long; Be-
4. And ye, beneath life's crushing load, Whose forms are bending low, Who
5. For lo! the days are hast'ning on, By prophet bards foretold, When

angels bending near the earth, To touch their harps of gold; "Peace
still their heavenly music floats O'er all the weary world; A-
neath the angel strain have rolled Two thousand years of wrong; And
toil along the climbing way With painful steps and slow, Look
with the ever circling years Comes round the age of gold; When

on the earth, good will to men, From Heav'en's all gracious King." The
bove its sad and lowly plains, They bend on hov'ring wing, And
man, at war with man, hears not The love-song which they bring; O
now! for glad and golden hours Come swiftly on the wing. O
peace shall over all the earth Its ancient splendors fling, And

world in solemn stillness lay, To hear the angels sing.
ever over its Babel sounds The blessed angels sing.
hush the noise, ye men of strife And hear the angels sing.
rest beside the weary road, And hear the angels sing!
the whole world send back the song Which now the angels sing.

Joy to the World

Isaac Watts, 1719

Remember back to Genesis 3, the tragic moment in salvation history, when Adam and Eve sinned against God and the relationship between God and His creation was ruptured. But there was hope; it was foretold that a woman would bear a son who would crush the head of the serpent (see Gen 3:15). Now, that Lord is come! Psalm 98:4 says, "Make a joyful noise to the Lord, all the earth" because God has come to restore His creation!

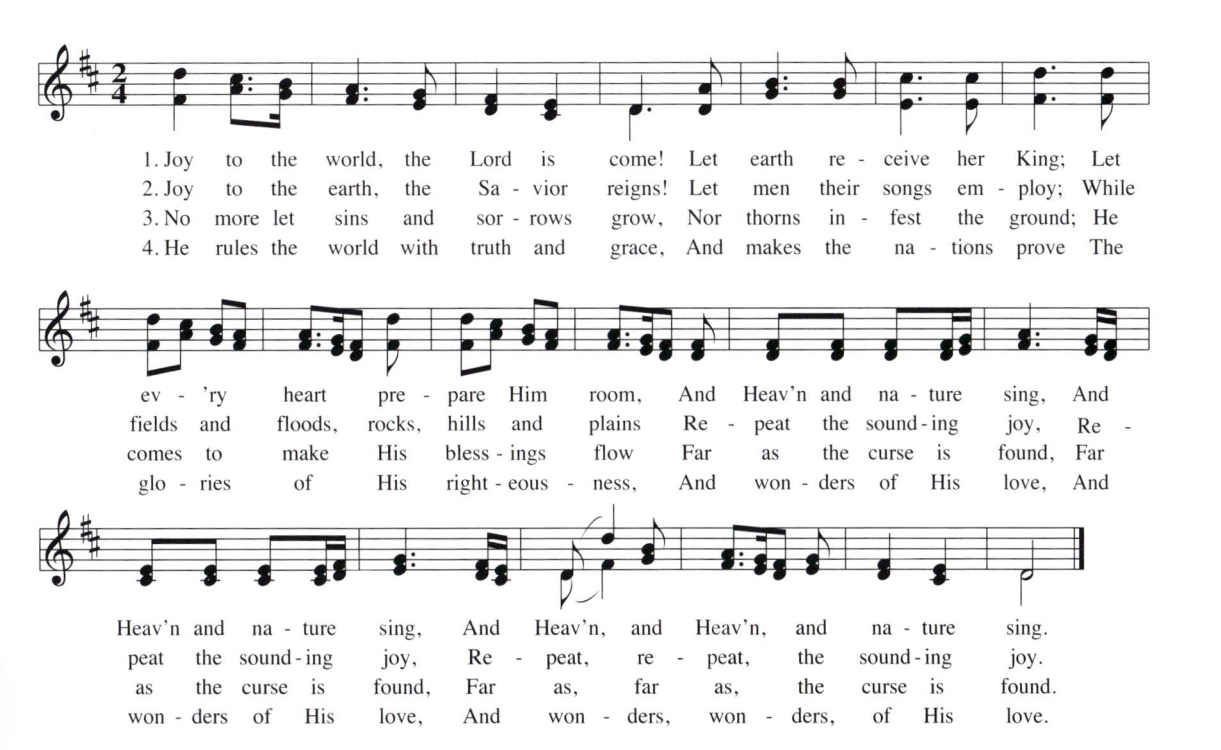

1. Joy to the world, the Lord is come! Let earth re-ceive her King; Let ev-'ry heart pre-pare Him room, And Heav'n and na-ture sing, And Heav'n and na-ture sing, And Heav'n, and Heav'n, and na-ture sing.

2. Joy to the earth, the Sa-vior reigns! Let men their songs em-ploy; While fields and floods, rocks, hills and plains Re-peat the sound-ing joy, Re-peat the sound-ing joy, Re-peat, re-peat, the sound-ing joy.

3. No more let sins and sor-rows grow, Nor thorns in-fest the ground; He comes to make His bless-ings flow Far as the curse is found, Far as the curse is found, Far as, far as, the curse is found.

4. He rules the world with truth and grace, And makes the na-tions prove The glo-ries of His right-eous-ness, And won-ders of His love, And won-ders of His love, And won-ders, won-ders, of His love.

O Come, All Ye Faithful

Adeste Fideles

Attributed to John Francis Wade, 1751

It is hard to sing this carol without smiling! There is such excitement in its earnestness. Hurry, hurry! Come, come! Greet the King of Angels, God of God and Light of Light, begotten not made, the Word made Flesh. "Great indeed, we confess, is the mystery of our religion: He was manifested in the flesh, vindicated in the Spirit, seen by angels, preached among the nations, believed on in the world, taken up in glory" (1 Tm 3:16). With great triumph, praise and adore Him with the angels and give thanks for His coming during this happy season.

The Word was made flesh, and dwelt among us. -Jn 1:14

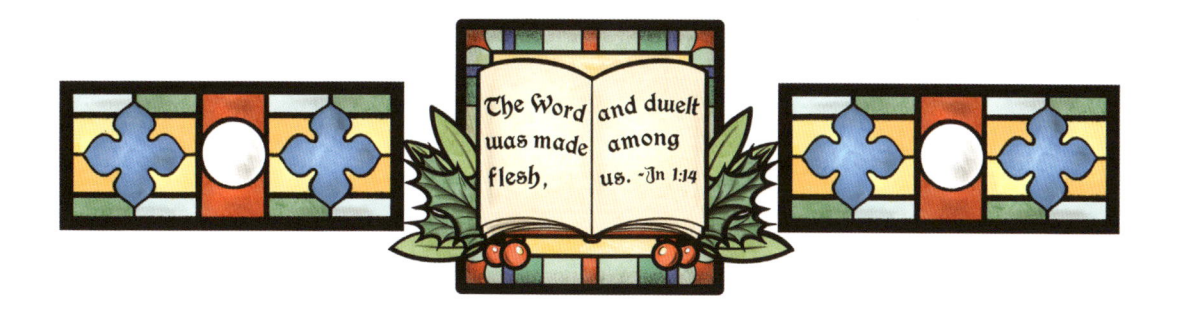

1. O come, all ye faith-ful, joy-ful and tri-um-phant, O come ye, O come ye, to Beth-le-hem. Come and be-hold Him, born the King of an-gels; O come, let us a-dore Him, O come, let us a-dore Him, O come, let us a-dore Him, Christ the Lord.

2. True God of true God, Light from Light E-ter-nal, Lo, He ab-hors not the Vir-gin's womb; Son of the Fa-ther, be-got-ten, not cre-a-ted;

3. Sing, choirs of an-gels, sing in ex-ul-ta-tion; O sing, all ye cit-i-zens of heav'n a-bove! Glo-ry to God, glo-ry in the high-est;

1. Adeste fideles laeti triumpantes
   Venite, venite in Bethlehem;
   Natum videte, Regem Angelorum.

2. Æterni Parentis, spendorem æternum
   Velatum sub carne videbimus;
   Deum Infantem, pannis involutum.

Refrain: Venite adoremus,
Venite adoremus Dominum.

O Come, O Come, Emmanuel
Veni Veni Emmanuel

Latin, circa 12th Century
Translated by J. M. Neale

Sung during the season of Advent, this hymn catalogues the "O" Antiphons, a part of the liturgy which listed the Old Testament titles of the coming Messiah. Jesus—Wisdom Himself (Sir 24:3), the Lord and Ruler (Ex 3:14), the Root of Jesse (Is 11:1), the Key of David (Is 22:22), the Rising Dawn or Morning Star (Hb 3:4, Rv 22:16), the King of Nations (Jer 10:7), Emmanuel (Is 7:14) —has come to fulfill all of the Old Testament prophesies . . . and will come again someday. This Truth is an occasion for great rejoicing.

1. O come, O come, Emmanuel, And ransom captive Israel, That mourns in lonely exile here Until the Son of God appear. Rejoice! Rejoice! Emmanuel shall come to thee, O Israel.

2. O come, O Wisdom from on high, who orderest all things mightily; To us the path of knowledge show, and teach us in its ways to go.

3. O come, O come, great Lord of might, who to Your tribes on Sinai's height in ancient times did give the law in cloud and majesty and awe.

4. O come, O Branch of Jesse's stem, unto Your own and rescue them! From depths of hell your people save, and give them vict'ry o'er the grave.

5. O come, O Key of David, come and open wide our heav'nly home. Make safe for us the heavenward road and bar the way to death's abode.

6. O come, O Bright and Morning Star, and bring us comfort from afar! Dispel the shadows of the night and turn our darkness into light.

7. O come, O King of nations, bind in one the hearts of all mankind. Bid all our sad divisions cease and be Yourself our King of Peace.

1. Veni, veni Emmanuel; Captivum solve Israel,
   Qui gemit in exilio, Privatus Dei Filio.

   Refrain: Gaude! Gaude! Emmanuel,
   Nascetur pro te, Israel!

2. Veni, O Iesse Virgula, Ex hostis tuos ungula,
   De spectu tuos tartari Educ et antro barathri.

3. Veni, veni, O Oriens; Solare nos adveniens,
   Noctis depelle nebulas, Dirasque noctis tenebras.

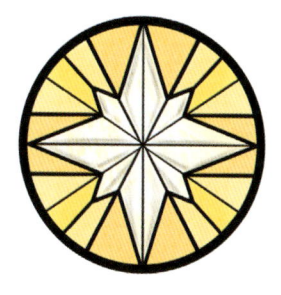

O Holy Night

Placide Cappeau (author), 1847
Translated by John Dwight, 1855

The soul feels its worth when it encounters Christ. It is He whom we were made for! As Saint Augustine wrote, in his *Confessions*, "Our hearts are restless, until they rest in You." No wonder the evening of His birth is such a holy one. On this night, the world meets its Savior face to face! He turns things upside down—kings bowing before a Baby, slaves as brothers—and thank God for that. Because we are not worthy of His love, yet He lavishes it upon us. Praise His name forever!

O holy night! The stars are brightly shining; It is the night of our dear Savior's birth. Long lay the world in sin and error pining, Till He appeared and the soul felt its worth. A thrill of hope, the weary world rejoices, For yonder breaks a new and glorious morn! Fall on your knees! O hear the angel voices! O night divine, O night when Christ was born! O night, O holy night, O night divine!

O Little Town of Bethlehem

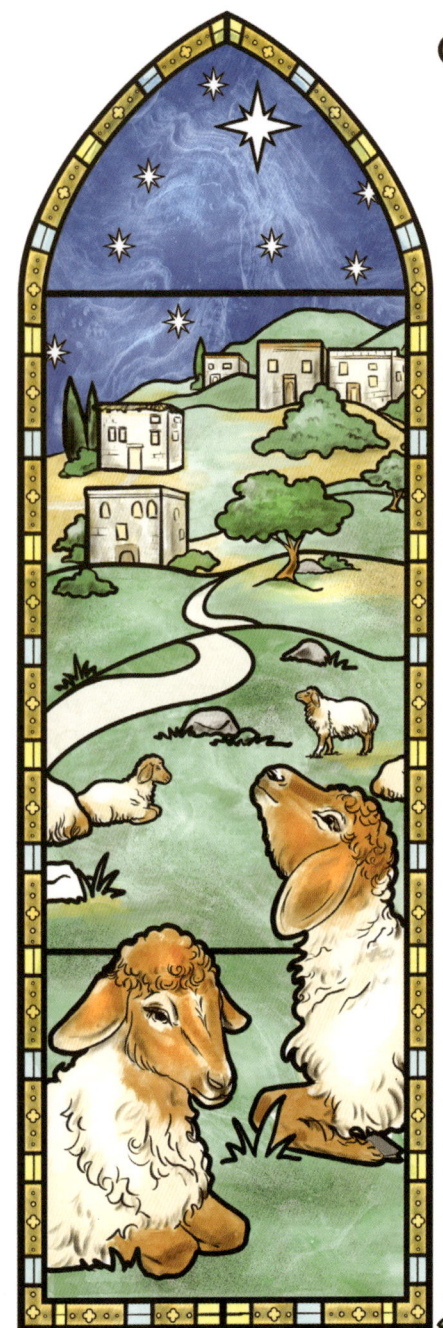

Phillips Brooks, 1868

Can you hear it? The silence and stillness of Bethlehem at night—stars quietly twinkling in the sky, people sleeping throughout the town—no one yet realizing that in a simple animal manger, "when the time had fully come, God sent forth his Son, born of woman" (Gal 4:4), a humble handmaid named Mary. While many hymns remind us of the grandeur of the angels' song of *Gloria*, this carol points out how the greater world around Him was largely ignorant of His coming on that holy night. "Thanks be to God for his inexpressible gift"! (2 Cor 9:15)

1. O little town of Bethlehem, how still we see thee lie! Above thy deep and dreamless sleep the silent stars go by. Yet in thy dark streets shineth the everlasting Light; The hopes and fears of all the years are met in thee tonight.

2. For Christ is born of Mary, and gathered all above, While mortals sleep, the angels keep their watch of won'dring love. O morning stars together, proclaim the holy birth, And praises sing to God the King, and peace to men on earth!

3. How silently, how silently, the wondrous Gift is giv'n; So God imparts to human hearts the blessings of His Heav'n. No ear may hear His coming, but in this world of sin, Where meek souls will receive Him still, the dear Christ enters in.

4. Where children pure and happy pray to the blessed Child, Where misery cries out to Thee, Son of the mother mild; Where charity stands watching and faith holds wide the door, The dark night wakes, the glory breaks, and Christmas comes once more.

5. O holy Child of Bethlehem, descend to us, we pray; Cast out our sin, and enter in, be born in us today. We hear the Christmas angels the great glad tidings tell; O come to us, abide with us, our Lord Emmanuel!

Once in Royal David's City

Cecil Frances Alexander, 1848

From heaven to earth and back again, this hymn shows us the interplay between Christ's humanity and divinity, His heavenly origins and earthly mission: His showcase of redeeming love. He now sits at the right hand of the Father in glory, beckoning us to join Him! "Beloved, we are God's children now . . . we know that when he appears we shall be like him, for we shall see him as he is" (1 Jn 3:2).

1 Once in ro - yal Da - vid's ci - ty stood a low - ly cat - tle shed, where a
2 He came down to earth from hea - ven who is God and Lord of all, and his
3 Je - sus is our chil - dhood's pat - tern, day by day like us he grew; he was
4 And our eyes at last shall see him, through his own re - deem - ing love; for that

mo - ther laid her ba - by in a man - ger for his bed: Ma - ry
shel - ter was a sta - ble, and his cra - dle was a stall: with the
lit - tle, weak, and help - less, tears and smiles like us he knew: and he
child, so dear and gen - tle, is our Lord in heaven a - bove: and he

was that mo - ther mild, Je - sus Christ her lit - tle
poor and meek and low - ly lived on earth, our Sa - vior
feels for all our sad - ness, and he shares in all our
leads his chil - dren on to the place where he has

child.
ho - ly.
glad - ness.
gone.

5. Not in that poor lowly stable, with the oxen standing by,
we shall see Him, but in heaven, set at God's right hand on high;
when like stars His children crowned all in white shall wait around.

Silent Night

Joseph Mohr, Franz Gruber, 1818

Psalm 46:10 reads, "Be still, and know that I am God." Imagine the presence of God piercing the silent night of Christmas. The thought should bring chills, a sense of awe and inexpressible wonder. Let the words of this wildly popular Christmas carol not fall on empty ears and hearts. "The Word became flesh and dwelt among us" (Jn 1:14).

1. Si - lent night, ho - ly night, All is calm, all is bright
Round yon vir - gin mo - ther and Child. Ho - ly In - fant, so ten - der and mild,
Sleep in hea - ven - ly peace, Sleep in hea - ven - ly peace.

2. Si - lent night, ho - ly night, Shep - herds quake at the sight;
Glo - ries stream from hea - ven a - far, Heaven - ly hosts sing Al - le - lu - ia!
Christ the Sa - vior is born, Christ the Sa - vior is born!

3. Si - lent night, ho - ly night, Son of God, love's pure light;
Ra - diant beams from Thy ho - ly face With the dawn of re - deem - ing grace,
Je - sus, Lord, at Thy birth, Je - sus, Lord, at Thy birth.

4. Si - lent night, ho - ly night Won - drous star, lend thy light;
With the an - gels let us sing, Al - le - lu - ia to our King;
Christ the Sa - vior is born, Christ the Sa - vior is born!

The First Noel

English Carol, 17th Century

Noel or *nowell* means "Christmas" or "to be born, birth." As if right out of the Gospels (Matthew 2 and Luke 2), this beautiful hymn recounts the birth of Christ on that peaceful, glorious night. You can almost see the stars twinkling with the pace and cadence of the song. As the wise men followed and revered, so let us follow the Christ Child, not just to meet Him at Christmas, but to follow Him all the days of our lives, wherever He may lead.

1. The first No - el the an - gel did say Was to cer - tain poor shep-herds in
2. They look - èd up and saw a star Shin-ing in the east, be -
3. And by the light of that same star Three Wise Men came from
4. This star drew nigh to the north - west, Ov - er Beth - le - hem it
5. Then did they know as - sur - ed - ly With - in that house the

fields as they lay; In fields where they lay tend - ing their sheep, On a
yond them far; And to where the earth it gave great light, And
coun - try far; To seek for a King was their in - tent, And to
took its rest; And there it did both stop and stay, Right
King did lie; One en - tered it them for to see, And

cold win - ter's night that was so deep. No - el, No -
so it con - tin - ued both day and night.
fol - low the star wher - ev - er it went.
ov - er the place where Je - sus lay.
found the Babe in pov - er - ty.

el, No - el, No - el, Born is the King of Is - ra - el.

What Child Is This?

William Chatterton Dix, 1865

Isaiah 9:6 proclaims, "For to us a child is born, to us a son is given; and the government will be upon his shoulder, and his name will be called 'Wonderful Counselor, Mighty God, Everlasting Father, Prince of Peace.'" The Christ Child is such a paradox—a Person both small and mighty, an Infant resting in a mother's lap and still a King, guarded and lauded. Jesus reminds us, even from the moment of His birth, that God's ways are not ours. "But God chose what is foolish in the world to shame the wise, God chose what is weak in the world to shame the strong, God chose what is low and despised in the world, even things that are not, to bring to nothing things that are, so that no human being might boast in the presence of God" (1 Cor 1:27–29).

1. What Child is this who, laid to rest On Mary's lap, is sleeping? Whom
2. Why lies He in such mean estate, Where ox and ass are feeding? Good
3. So bring Him incense, gold and myrrh, Come peasant, king to own Him; The

angels greet with anthems sweet, While shepherds watch are keeping?
Christians, fear, for sinners here The silent Word is pleading.
King of kings salvation brings, Let loving hearts enthrone Him.

This, this is Christ the King, Whom shepherds guard and angels sing;

Haste, haste, to bring Him laud, The Babe, the Son of Mary.

We Three Kings of Orient Are

John H. Hopkins, Jr., 1857

May our singing of this carol aid us in reflecting on the Magi's journey to Bethlehem—one which traversed great distance and various terrains, for such a worthy purpose: to meet the truest King whom ever lived. The verses enlighten us to the meaning of their gifts: gold for Christ's kingship or royalty; frankincense for His deity or divinity; and myrrh, a symbol of death or mortality.

1. We three kings of O - ri - ent are; bear - ing gifts we tra - verse a - far,
2. Born a King on Beth - le-hem's plain, gold I bring to crown him a - gain,
3. Frank - in - cense to of - fer have I; in - cense owns a De - i - ty nigh;
4. Myrrh is mine; its bit - ter per - fume breathes a life of ga - the - ring gloom;
5. Glo - rious now be - hold him a - rise; King and God and sac - ri - fice:

field and foun - tain, moor and moun - tain, fol - lo - wing yon - der star.
King for - e - ver, ceas - ing ne - ver, o - ver us all to reign.
prayer and prais - ing, voi - ces rais - ing, wor - shi - ping God on high.
sorrow - ing, sigh - ing, bleed - ing, dy - ing, sealed in the stone-cold tomb.
Al - le - lu - ia, Al - le - lu - ia, sounds through the earth and skies.

Refrain

O_____ star of won - der, star of light, star with roy - al beau - ty bright,

west - ward lead - ing, still pro - ceed - ing, guide us to thy per - fect light.

We consider Christmas as the encounter, the great encounter, the historical encounter, the decisive encounter, between God and mankind. He who has faith knows this truly; let him rejoice.

—St. Paul VI

Katie Warner is a Catholic homeschooling mom and a bestselling children's book author. Her popular titles include *Oremus: Latin Prayers for Young Catholics* and *One Holy Marriage: The Story of Saints Louis and Zelie Martin*. She has a graduate degree in Catholic Theology and lives in Georgia with her husband and fellow book-loving children. Check out her entire children's book collection at FirstFaithTreasury.com, and connect with Katie online (she loves to hear from readers!) at KatieWarner.com or @katiewarnercatholic.

Adalee Hude, a wife, mother to two beautiful adopted children (and several wee intercessors), and Catholic author and artist, runs Brightly Hude Studio. Fueled largely by prayer and tea, she has done illustration work for Catholic magazines, prayer journals, stickers, and several children's books. Her own books include *Sanctus, Sanctus, Sanctus: An Introductory Latin Missal for Children*, published by TAN Books, and *Light of Heaven: A Children's Book of Saints*, published by OSV. Find out more at brightlyhude.com. AMDG!